Handbook of Scriptural Novenas

For various needs and intentions

by
Glynn MacNiven-Johnston
& Raymond Edwards

*All booklets are published thanks to the
generous support of the members of the
Catholic Truth Society*

CATHOLIC TRUTH SOCIETY
PUBLISHERS TO THE HOLY SEE

Contents

What is a Novena? 3

How to use this booklet 6

Moses - discerning and accepting our vocation 7

Elijah - finding strength in God 15

Tobit - Marriage 23

Hannah - the gift of children 31

Joseph & his brothers - for peace in the family 36

David & Absalom and the Prodigal Son
- estranged children 43

Martha - being the one that does all the work 50

Ruth and Naomi - feeling abandoned and forgotten . . 56

Deborah and Barak
- when things seem too much for us. 62

Jonah - when God's plan doesn't seem to make sense. . 68

Job - being honest with God. 75

Abraham - old age 83

All rights reserved. First published 2015 by The Incorporated Catholic Truth Society, 40-46 Harleyford Road London SE11 5AY Tel: 020 7640 0042 Fax: 020 7640 0046. © 2015 The Incorporated Catholic Truth Society.

ISBN 978 1 78469 066 3

What is a Novena?

A novena is a way of praying, often for a particular need or grace. It consists of a prayer or prayers said over nine days. The word *novena* is originally Latin, and means "in a group of nine".[1] This is because a novena lasts for nine consecutive days; on each day, there is a particular prayer to be said, or devotional practice to be made.

The original novena, the model for all the rest, is the nine days between Christ's Ascension and the descent of the Holy Spirit at Pentecost, when, as we read in the Acts of the Apostles, "all these [Apostles] joined in continuous prayer, together with several women, including Mary the mother of Jesus".[2] The Church still asks Christians to pray with particular intensity between these two feast days for the Holy Spirit to renew the Christian community.[3]

There are many different sorts of novena; you can make a novena using any prayer you want: the main thing is to pray it regularly for nine days in a row. Nevertheless most people will make a novena using a prayer composed for the purpose. Some novena prayers are long, and may include litanies, or meditations; others are short. You can make a novena using the same prayer nine times, or nine different prayers, one for each day. There are no rules; what follows are only suggestions.

Many novenas (including those in the companion volume *Handbook of Novenas to the Saints* (CTS, 2010)) ask the intercession of a particular saint for whatever our intention may be. As well as interceding (praying) on our behalf, the saints are also examples of how the Christian life has been lived. Each saint experienced different events, and responded to them in different ways; we can see in their lives examples of how embracing God's will for us, whatever our individual circumstances, always brings the grace and strength from God we need to do what he asks us. To use religious language, the saints are examples of particular virtues.

The novenas in this book are slightly different. They focus on particular figures from the Bible, most from the Old Testament (the Hebrew Scriptures) because from the start, the Christian life has been lived after the model of the Old Covenant.[4] Scripture is a record of God's mighty deeds with his people, which are the pattern for his deeds with us today. Biblical figures are not given to us for our imitation, not in all the details of their lives (King David was a murderer and an adulterer, Jacob deceived his father and cheated his brother, Jonah was grumpy and rebellious) but rather in one particular - their ability to accept, often after a struggle, the action of God in their lives, and his will for them. This acceptance, however it was mediated and however it played out, allowed their lives to assume a particular shape and conform to the providential pattern

God intended. In this way, they become images - icons, types - of particular virtues or characteristics - Abraham of faith, Job of perseverance amidst suffering - and it is their whole-hearted, even if grudging and gradual, giving permission for God's act that makes them not just characters in a historical narrative (although they retain that historical identity and function) but exemplars of a living faith for us today.

By bringing our own questions, troubles, needs, despair or hope to God in the context of these patterned lives, we are inviting God to act with us as he did for them. Sometimes our circumstances may be similar to theirs - Job despairing in the ruins of his life, Hannah asking for children; sometimes our apparent circumstances may be very different, but underneath this, our disposition may be identical. We are unlikely to find ourselves actually stuck between an Egyptian army and the impassable waters of the Red Sea, but we may well find ourselves trapped between apparently inescapable problems. God opened a way for Moses and the Israelites; he will open one for us, if we ask him with faith. God keeps his promises; and he is stronger than death.

In the novena prayers that follow here, we have tried for each day to take one particular virtue or quality or response that a scriptural character (or characters) has shown, and ask God to make it our own too, according to our needs and circumstances; and in this context we can pray for any particular intention we may have, whether for ourselves or for another.

How to use this booklet

Each novena in this booklet focuses on one or more figures from the Bible. You may want to read the relevant passages from Scripture, so at the start of each novena we have said where these can be found. You do not have to read these passages before making a novena; but you may find it helpful. Then each novena is arranged into nine days. For each day, there is a short passage of Scripture, then a short reflection and prayer.

On each day of the novena, say these, and add your particular intention, if you have one; then say the Our Father, the Hail Mary, and the Glory Be. Do this on each of the nine days.

You may find it helpful to keep a short time of silence after reading the passage from Scripture. Scripture is the Word of God; God speaks to us through it. But to hear what he wants to say to us, we need to be quiet and listen. We may have much to say to God; he surely has something to say to us.

MOSES - DISCERNING AND
ACCEPTING OUR VOCATION

Scripture: *read the story of Moses*
(*Exodus 1-20, 32-4, Deuteronomy*)

B esides Abraham, Moses is perhaps the clearest example
Scripture gives of God acting in one man's life. Moses
is a reluctant prophet; but he accepts,
eventually, that God has a purpose for
him, and follows his call even though it
sometimes looks to him, and to others,
like plain lunacy. He is not a plaster saint
- he is angry, impatient, mistrustful of
God and himself, prone to doubt; yet he also trusts that
God will fulfil his promises, and so becomes the means for
God to achieve literally incredible things.

First Day: *Now Pharoah's daughter went down to bathe
in the river...Among the reeds she noticed a basket...She
opened it, and saw a baby boy, crying; and she was sorry for
him* (*Ex* 2:5-6)

Pharaoh planned to kill all male Hebrew children; God
intervened to frustrate this plan in several ways. Moses

was, ironically, rescued by Pharaoh's own daughter. God had a plan for him. We are unlikely to know all the details, but we may feel sure that God's providence has preserved us, too, from our childhood.

❖ Father, help me to believe that you have a plan for me, too. Help me to be thankful for those parts of your plan I can already see. I pray especially for (name your intention)

Our Father - Hail Mary - Glory Be

Second Day: *Moses, a man by now...saw an Egyptian strike a Hebrew, one of his countrymen. Looking round, he could see no one, so he killed the Egyptian and hid him in the sand...When Pharaoh heard of the matter he would have killed Moses, but Moses fled from Pharaoh and made for the land of Midian.* (Ex 2:11-12, 15)

Moses is a man of high status in Egypt, but he feels sympathy for his own people, who are oppressed. But his first rash effort to help them is a disaster, and he has to run away. We too can try to force God's hand by acting rashly; this usually turns out badly.

❖ Father, help me to be patient; but also to know remember that you can repair whatever mistakes I have made: your plans are not defeated by my impatience. I pray especially for (name your intention)

Our Father - Hail Mary - Glory Be

Third Day: *Moses...led his flock to the far side of the wilderness and came to Horeb, the mountain of God. There, the angel of the Lord appeared to him in the shape of a flame of fire, coming from the middle of a bush..."I must go and look at this strange sight," Moses said...and God called to him from the middle of the bush..."Come no nearer," he said. "Take off your shoes, for the place on which you stand is holy ground."* (3:1-5)

Moses did not expect to be called by God in this way, amidst his laborious daily round. Yet he was open to hearing God's voice, and knew that any place and time is made holy when God acts there.

❖ Father, help me be attentive to the signs you send, and open to your presence and action where I do not expect it, and especially in the midst of my daily life. I pray especially for (name your intention)

Our Father - Hail Mary - Glory Be

Fourth Day: *And the Lord said "I have seen the miserable state of my people in Egypt...so come, I send you to Pharaoh to bring the sons of Israel, my people, out of Egypt." Moses said to God, "Who am I to go to Pharaoh and bring the sons of Israel out of Egypt?"* (4:7, 10-11)

Like Moses, we may not believe we are able to be called in the way that God seems to be calling us (as a priest, or a husband, or mother, or whatever it might be). We need to trust that God will help us to do what we are given to do. St Catherine of Siena said, "Be what you are meant to be, and you will set the entire world alight".

❖ Father, help me to trust that you know what you are doing. I pray especially for (name your intention)

Our Father - Hail Mary - Glory Be

Fifth Day: *And as Pharaoh approached…the sons of Israel were terrified…To Moses they said, "Were there no graves in Egypt that you must lead us out to die in the wilderness?"… The Lord said to Moses "Tell the sons of Israel to march on."* (14:10-11, 15)

After many miraculous signs from God, Pharaoh finally lets the people of Israel go, only to change his mind soon after and pursue them. Moses and the Israelites are caught between the impassable sea and a pursuing army. We too may know what it is like to feel trapped, helpless, terrified, whether by circumstances or by our own sins; but the same God who opened a way for the Israelites through the sea can open one for us, and will, if only we ask him in faith.

❖ Father, I ask for the faith to make this prayer. I pray especially for (name your intention)

Our Father - Hail Mary - Glory Be

Sixth Day: *When the people saw that Moses was a long time before coming down the mountain, they gathered round Aaron and said to him, "Come, make us a god..." He cast an effigy of a calf. "Here is your God, Israel," they cried "who brought you out of the land of Egypt!" (32:1, 4)*

God gives the Law to Moses on Mount Sinai; but the Israelites, impatient at his absence, persuade Aaron to make them a visible idol, a golden calf (a typical pagan symbol of that time). When Moses sees this, he is furious, and in his frustration throws down the tablets of the Law. Yet he does not give up on the Israelites.

❖ I am often impatient of the imperfections and faults of those I have to work with. But, Father, you have put us together for a reason; help me to trust you know what you are doing. These are never the people I would have designed or chosen, but (in the end) that is a very good thing. I pray especially for (name your intention)

Our Father - Hail Mary - Glory Be

Seventh Day: *Moses pleaded with the Lord his God. "Lord," he said "why should your wrath blaze out against this people of yours whom you brought out of the land of Egypt with arm outstretched and mighty hand...Remember Abraham, Isaac and Jacob, your servants to whom by your own self you swore..." So the Lord relented and did not bring on his people the disaster he had threatened. (32:11, 13-14)*

Despite his frustration with the people, Moses keeps praying to God on the mountain, interceding for Israel. His appeal for them turns aside God's anger, and saves them. God does not need our prayer, but he has chosen to grant us a share in his own creative and sustaining work; and one big way we do this is by praying. We need to keep praying, even if we cannot see any results, or if the thing we are praying for (for us or for someone else) seems to be constantly withheld or taken away. We cannot see more than a tiny fraction of the patterned causes that enfold the world and ourselves, let alone judge what effect our small efforts are having.

❖ Father, help me to believe you will turn my prayers to good account, however poor or meaningless they sometimes seem. I pray especially for (name your intention)

Our Father - Hail Mary - Glory Be

Eighth Day: *And the Lord said to Moses: "How long will this people insult me? How long will they refuse to believe in me despite the signs I have worked among them? I will strike them with pestilence and disown them."…Moses answered the Lord… "No, my Lord! It is now you must display your power, according to those words you spoke, 'the Lord is slow to anger and rich in graciousness, forgiving faults and transgressions…' In the abundance, then, of your graciousness, forgive the sin of this people." (Nb 14:11-13, 17-19)*

The journey of Israel to the Promised Land takes forty long years, and takes them through many trials and hardships. They repeatedly complain and blame Moses and the Lord for all this, and often lapse into paganism. But Moses, although frustrated, does not give up on them, and reminds God of his promise.

❖ Father, help me likewise to persevere in what I have begun, despite the hardships of the journey, and to remember all you have done for me, and that you are faithful to your promises. I pray especially for (name your intention)

Our Father - Hail Mary - Glory Be

Ninth Day: *"The Lord has been angry with me on your account; he has sworn that I shall not cross the Jordan or enter the prosperous land which the Lord your God is giving you as your heritage...Take care therefore not to forget the covenant which the Lord your God has made with you...for the Lord your God is a consuming fire, a jealous God...But if you seek him with all your heart and with all your soul, you shall find him...for the Lord your God is a merciful God and will not desert or destroy you or forget the covenant he made on oath with your fathers."* (Dt 4:21, 23-24, 29, 31)

Moses is held responsible for the people's sins, and so cannot enter the Promised Land; he accepts this suffering for the sake of the people, and testifies to the enduring faithfulness of God.

❖ Father, help me to accept whatever suffering you give me, for the salvation of others, as did Moses, and your Son Jesus Christ; help me to know and to trust your enduring love and mercy towards me. I pray especially for (name your intention) .

Our Father - Hail Mary - Glory Be

ELIJAH - FINDING STRENGTH IN GOD

Scripture: *read the story of Elijah*
(*1 Kings* 17-22, *2 Kings* 1-2)

Elijah is the great hero-prophet of the Israelite kingdom. He witnesses above all to the need to worship God alone (his name means "my God is the Lord") in a world saturated with pagan idols. He is fearless in confronting the prophets of Baal, and standing up to the wickedness of King Ahab and his wife Jezebel. But after his triumph over false prophets, he is terrified by the king's threats, and overwhelmed by what God is asking him to do. He wishes he were dead. We too, however much we have achieved, often can feel utterly crushed by the tasks that keep coming to us - work, children, elderly parents, illness, all the myriad difficulties and responsibilities we have. God renews Elijah's strength, however, and then leads him to Mount Horeb, where he hears God's voice in the gentle breeze. Then he returns to call Israel, and especially its wicked rulers, to turn to God again.

First Day: *Elijah the Tishbite...said to Ahab, "As the Lord lives, the God of Israel whom I serve, there shall be neither dew nor rain these years except at my order". The word of the Lord came to him, "Go away from here...and hide yourself in the wadi Cherith which lies east of Jordan...He did as the Lord had said...The ravens brought him bread in the morning and meat in the evening, and he quenched his thirst at the stream. (17:1-3, 5-6)*

The people of Israel, led by their king Ahab, turned from God to the worship of idols. It was left to Elijah alone to bear witness to God, and to call the king to repent. God made Elijah a promise to keep him alive in the drought that was the sign of God's displeasure.

❖ Father, you know how trying to live by your word is sometimes difficult, and how living as a Christian in the world can seem lonely or irrational. Help me to trust that if I witness to your love for all people, you will support me. I pray especially for (name your intention)

Our Father - Hail Mary - Glory Be

Second Day: *The word of the Lord came to him, "Up and go to Zarephath, a Sidonian town, and stay there. I have ordered a widow there to give you food." (17:8-9)*

God sends Elijah to live in a pagan town; there, he works great signs through him - first, he provides food for the widow, her son, and Elijah; then he raises the widow's son from the dead.

❖ Father, help me to see that you are at work amongst all people, not just those visibly within the Church; help me be a sign to them of your love that is stronger than death, and let me not forget that they, too, can be the means of your care for me. I pray especially for (name your intention)

Our Father - Hail Mary - Glory Be

Third Day: *The word of the Lord came to Elijah…"Go, present yourself to Ahab…" So Elijah set off to present himself to Ahab…When he saw Elijah, Ahab said, "So there you are, you scourge of Israel!" "Not I," he replied. "I am not the scourge of Israel, you and your family are; because you have deserted the Lord." (1 K 18:1-2, 17-18)*

Ahab's wife, Jezebel, had killed all of the Lord's prophets she could find, and Ahab had scoured all the country and its neighbours looking for Elijah, to kill him also. But Elijah, strong in his faith in God, is fearless.

❖ Father, help me not to be afraid to acknowledge you, to confront whatever in my life I fear to meet, and to speak the truth although I know it may not be welcome; give me faith in your saving help. I pray especially for (name your intention)

Our Father - Hail Mary - Glory Be

Fourth Day: *Elijah stepped out in front of all the people. "How long" he said "do you mean to hobble first on one leg then on the other? If the Lord is God, follow him; if Baal, follow him." But the people never said a word.* (18:21)

The people of Israel were reluctant to trust themselves wholly to God, and (like their neighbours) were prone to pay their respects as well to the gods of the locality, either following the example of their kings, or as a form of supernatural insurance policy. We should not think we are immune from this temptation.

❖ Father, you know how hard I find it to trust your providence, your plan for my life, and how tempted I am to try to hedge my bets and make bargains with the world and its idols. Help me to trust you and to know you will not fail me. I pray especially for (name your intention)

Our Father - Hail Mary - Glory Be

Fifth Day: *Elijah climbed to the top of Carmel and bowed down to the earth, putting his face between his knees. "Now go up," he told his servant "and look out to the sea." He went up and looked. "There is nothing at all" he said. "Go back seven times" Elijah said. The seventh time, the servant said, "Now there is a cloud, small as a man's hand, rising from the sea."* (18:42-44)

Elijah trusted in God's word to him, and persevered in looking for the sign he knew God would send that salvation - rain after drought - was coming to Israel.

❖ Father, help me to be patient in discerning the signs of your work for myself and for others. I pray especially for (name your intention)

Our Father - Hail Mary - Glory Be

Sixth Day: *Elijah said, "Go and say to Ahab, 'Harness the chariot and go down before the rain stops you'". And with that the sky grew dark with cloud and storm, and rain fell in torrents. Ahab mounted his chariot and made for Jezreel. The hand of the Lord was on Elijah, and tucking up his cloak he ran in front of Ahab as far as the outskirts of Jezreel.* (18:44-46)

Surely one of the most striking images in Scripture is this, the prophet Elijah running through a rain-storm the sixteen miles or so between Mount Carmel and Jezreel, outpacing the king's chariot, the skies dark and thunderous, rain loud on the dry earth.

❖ Father, grant me your strength, and the faith you gave the prophet. I pray especially for (name your intention)

Our Father - Hail Mary - Glory Be

Seventh Day: *Elijah went on out into the wilderness, and sitting under a furze bush wished he were dead. "O Lord" he said, "I have had enough. Take my life; I am no better than my ancestors." Then he lay down and went to sleep. But an angel touched him and said, "Get up and eat." (1 K 19:4-5)*

After Elijah defeats the prophets of Baal, Ahab's queen, Jezebel, vows again to kill him. After his moment of triumph, he is exhausted and terrified, and flees. But God comes to him in a simple practical way - bringing food, and sleep.

❖ Father, help me to accept gratefully your great gifts of food and rest; help me not to give up, not to mistake fatigue, or the distorted gaze that sadness can bring, for the truth about the world and my place in it. Give me hope. I pray especially for (name your intention)

Our Father - Hail Mary - Glory Be

Eighth Day: *Then he was told, "Go and stand on the mountain before the Lord." Then the Lord himself went by. There came a mighty wind, so strong it tore the mountains and shattered the rocks before the Lord. But the Lord was not in the wind. After the wind came an earthquake. But the Lord was not in the earthquake. After the earthquake came a fire. But the Lord was not in the fire. And after the fire there came the sound of a gentle breeze. And when Elijah* *heard this, he covered his face with his cloak and went out and stood at the entrance to the cave. Then a voice came to him, which said, "What are you doing here, Elijah?"* (1 K 19:11-13)

Elijah, as we have seen, is at the end of his tether; he is once more convinced he alone in Israel has not abandoned God. But he follows a call to go to Horeb, the mountain of God. There, God does not show himself as a mighty force of nature, but as a quiet voice, which tells Elijah he is not alone, and has not been abandoned.

❖ Father, help me to listen patiently for your voice, not to rush to judgement or to mistake other things for you. Help me to make time for prayer. I pray especially for (name your intention)

Our Father - Hail Mary - Glory Be

Ninth Day: *Now as they walked on, talking as they went, a chariot of fire appeared and horses of fire, coming between the two of them; and Elijah went up to heaven in the whirlwind. Elisha saw it, and shouted, "My father! My father! Chariot of Israel and its chargers!"* (2 K 2:11-12)

Elijah is taken up in a fiery chariot; in the Gospels, he is one of the witnesses to the Transfiguration, and in both Jewish and Christian tradition will announce the Messiah's coming. He reminds us that we live in hope, not just of

God's action on our behalf in this life, but of his triumphant consummation and reconciling of all things at the end of time.

❖ Father, give me hope that you will make all things new. I pray especially for (name your intention)

Our Father - Hail Mary - Glory Be

TOBIT - MARRIAGE

Scripture: *read the Book of Tobit*

We may have many reasons to pray about marriage. If we are married, we may be experiencing difficulties - with our spouse or our children, or with money or where we are living or with some other aspect of our relationship. We may be unmarried, and want to ask God for a wife or a husband; we may be in a relationship, or even engaged to be married, and want God's help in discerning what to do now.

This novena draws on texts from the Book of Tobit. This book is conventionally listed amongst the historical books of the Bible, but it is actually what we would call a historical novel. It is set in the time of the Jewish exile in Babylon, although it was written much later. It tells the story of Tobit and his son Tobias, and how they are saved from various afflictions by God's angel Raphael. A big part of the story concerns Tobias's finding a wife, his distant cousin Sarah, and their triumph over adversity through God's help. Tobias and Sarah put all their difficulties into God's hands, and he does not let them down.

First Day: *Do not be afraid; she was destined for you from the beginning, and it is you who will save her.* (6:18)

Marriage is the sacramental means God has designed for the salvation of a human couple; each is the primary means, under God, of the other's salvation. Their physical bond is a covenanted means of grace for them. Spouses are indeed "destined for each other", but not in the sense that we need search the world for some supposed ideal person, "the One". God respects and confirms the choices we make, if we have discerned them with prayer and prudence. We should remember that all circumstances and events, even the apparently trivial, are from him; we should not be so daunted by them, or so fearful of risk, as to be afraid to act. God makes what we choose generously and lovingly into our "destiny"; his grace goes before us and after us.

❖ Father, we entrust our lives and marriage to you. Be with us in our joys and sorrows, and help us to see your hand even in what look like impossible difficulties. Take away all that stands in the way of our love for each other and for you. We pray especially for (name your intention)

Our Father - Hail Mary - Glory Be

Second Day: *He fell so deeply in love with her that he could no longer call his heart his own.* (6:18)

Marriage calls us to a total gift of our selves - heart, body, will - so that we no longer look first to our own good, but to that of our spouse, and (if God sends them) to that of our children. This gift of ourselves follows the pattern of the utter self-giving of the Holy Trinity, which is the very model of personhood: by living in this way, with God's grace, we become authentically human. Absolute self-giving in some form or other is part of the essential pattern of human happiness.

❖ Father, help us to give ourselves without reserve. We pray especially for (name your intention)

Our Father - Hail Mary - Glory Be

Third Day: *It was you who said, "It is not good that the man should be alone; let us make him a helpmate like himself." And so I do not take my sister for any lustful motive; I do it in singleness of heart.* (8:6-7)

Human beings are made to live in communion with each other. Physical attraction is a sign and an expression of this purpose, but (as fallen beings) we are sadly able to try to separate it from its proper context and make our proper physical desires just another way of being selfish. Sexuality is at the heart of any marriage, but needs to be part of our whole gift of ourselves in all our aspects ("singleness of heart").

❖ Father, help us to live our sexuality well, in love and truth. We pray especially for (name your intention)

Our Father - Hail Mary - Glory Be

Fourth Day: *Be kind enough to have pity on her and on me and bring us to old age together.* (8:7)

The real blessing of marriage lies not in the joys of courtship, the happiness of a wedding-day, or the delight of discovering life together, real and important though all these things are. It is in the gradual growth of the couple together, through whatever circumstances God sends them, so that they can be icons of Christ to each other and to the world; for this they need to accept the events, which may seem difficult or baffling, by which God remakes them together and slowly breaks down whatever may be in them that prevents the growth of love for God and for each other. Marriage requires us to give up self-will and live for the other; any honest reflection will admit this is a seemingly impossible task, but God is patient. For this he gives us a lifetime.

❖ Father, help us to welcome the events you send us, every day. We pray especially for (name your intention)

Our Father - Hail Mary - Glory Be

Fifth Day: *Tobias rose from the bed and said to Sarah, "Get up, my wife! You and I must pray and petition our Lord to win his grace and protection."* (8:4)

A married couple, or an engaged couple, should pray together. The world and the devil (which the Book of

Tobit personifies in the demon that afflicts Sarah before her marriage) set themselves against marriage, because a happy marriage is a living sign to the world of God's love. We need to pray for God to defend the possibility of marriage from all that would suggest to us that lifelong commitment is cruel or impossible. We should remember that, in marriage, we promise to stay with our spouse, and God promises to be with us to help us. And, unlike us, God always keeps his promises.

❖ Father, give us the spirit of prayer. We pray especially for (name your intention)

Our Father - Hail Mary - Glory Be

Sixth Day: *I must be frank with you: I have tried to find a husband for her seven times among our kinsmen, and all of them have died the first evening, on going to her room. But for the present, my boy, eat and drink; the Lord will grant you his grace and peace.* (7:10-11)

Sarah has been intended for marriage seven times already; on each occasion, her prospective husband has died before consummating the marriage. By rights, then, Tobias - who wants to marry her - is also a dead man. We may suppose, at times, that marriage means our death: death of that freedom to do what we want which we may think is characteristic of the single life. But Sarah's father has faith that God will protect Tobias; and he does. The "death" we may imagine lies in marriage will probably prove only an illusion; and, in any case, God has in Jesus Christ shown definitively that he is stronger than death.

❖ Father, help us not to be afraid. We pray especially for (name your intention)

Our Father - Hail Mary - Glory Be

Seventh Day: *Edna said to Tobias "Dear son...I hope to live long enough to see the children of you and my daughter Sarah...In the sight of the Lord I give my daughter into your keeping. Never make her unhappy as long as you live... Henceforward I am your mother..."* (10:12)

We should not think that relations with our parents-in-law will always be peaceful, or that it is always (or often) easy either for child or for parent to get used to the new relationships that marriage sets up. Both children and parents can find it difficult to detach, and to accept the new reality that, for the married couple, their spouse (and children, if God sends them) now holds the first place. But God is faithful, and can (and will) make all things new, if we trust him and ask him in faith.

❖ Father, help us to accept all the people you put in our life. We pray especially for (name your intention)

Our Father - Hail Mary - Glory Be

Eighth Day: *They laid [Tobit] back on his bed; he died and was buried with honour. When his mother died, Tobias buried her beside his father...Tobias...lived in Ecbatana with Raguel, his father-in-law. He treated the aging parents of his wife with every care and respect, and later buried them...Much honoured, he lived to the age of a hundred and seventeen years.* (14:11-14)

We may think the commandment "honour your father and mother, that you may have long life in the land" is a relic of an older form of society, and hardly applies to us now; we are perhaps inclined to be mildly amused that the author of Tobit seems to take it so literally. But the duty of care we owe to our parents is part of the wider duty we have to all who, like us, are children of the one Father. The fact that we know their faults better than most other people's doesn't exclude them from this. Marriage makes us more strongly incorporate into the Body of Christ, and part of a close-woven network of love that crosses the generations.

❖ Father, help us to live this truth. We pray especially for (name your intention)

Our Father - Hail Mary - Glory Be

Ninth Day: *Jerusalem, Holy City, God scourged you for your handiwork yet will still take pity on the sons of the upright... within you he may comfort every exile, and within you he may love all who are distressed, for all generations to come.*

*A bright light shall shine over all the regions of the earth;
many nations shall come from far away, from all the ends of
the earth, to dwell close to the holy name of the Lord God…
Within you, generation after generation shall proclaim their
joy.* (13:9-11)

All of our joys in this life are foretastes of the joy that God
will grant us in the fuller life to come, a life the author
of Tobit describes as the renewed Jerusalem. The love
and mutual forgiveness that God grants, in his grace, to
married couples and their children is a sign to the world of
this unimagined life, where all our promise will be fulfilled,
and our broken plans made whole.

❖ Father, help us to live the happiness we are given,
trusting that it is not an illusion, but a sign of what is to
come; and to accept whatever sufferings we are sent not as
punishment but as parts of a plan we cannot yet see, but
will, in your mercy, come some day to recognise. We pray
especially for (name your intention)

Our Father - Hail Mary - Glory Be

HANNAH - THE GIFT OF CHILDREN

Scripture: *read the story of Hannah* (*1 Samuel* 1:1-2:11)

The story of Hannah is found in the first book of Samuel. She is the prophet Samuel's mother; one of the two wives of Elkanah. Elkanah's other wife, Penninah, had children, but Hannah had none. In spite of this, Elkanah loved Hannah more than he loved Penninah, and perhaps because of this Penninah hated Hannah and taunted her for her childlessness. Hannah didn't insult Penninah back, but continued to pray to God. When the prophet Eli saw Hannah praying in the temple, he thought she was drunk; but Hannah remained humble. Finally her son Samuel was born. His name is said to mean "the Lord has heard". Hannah did not cling to the child, but gave him to serve God.

First Day: *Penninah had children but Hannah had none* (1:2)

❖ Father, you created me with the ability to give life. This desire is part of my being. You understand the longing I feel. Help me to trust in you; to know that you love me and do everything for my good. I bring this desire of mine before you, knowing you can fulfil it if you will; but let me enter into this novena trusting that if you do not give me what I hope for, it is out of love for me. Help me be at peace with this, not doubting your love but accepting all things in faith. I pray especially for (name your intention)

Our Father - Hail Mary - Glory Be

Second Day: *Her rival would taunt her to annoy her* (1:6)

Penninah had children, but she was still unhappy and jealous.

❖ Help me not to expect all my problems to be solved by having a child. Let me not want a child for purely selfish reasons: to heal my pride; to suck love from him or her; to fulfil my needs; to have my life as I planned it. Let me learn how to love as you do. I pray especially for (name your intention)

Our Father - Hail Mary - Glory Be

Third Day: *And this went on year after year. Every year when they went up to the Temple of the Lord she would taunt her.* (1:7)

Don't let me become jealous of those who have children.

❖ Don't let me judge them thinking I would be a better parent, and never allow me to judge you. Sometimes you give children to those who don't want them, or to those who mistreat them. Lord, I don't understand this. Give me the grace to know you don't make mistakes; that you love all those children more than I can understand, that their suffering grieves you deeply but that you can bring good even out of that evil. I pray especially for (name your intention)

Our Father - Hail Mary - Glory Be

Fourth Day: *Then Elkanah her husband said to her, "Hannah why are you crying and why are you not eating? Why so sad? Am I not more to you than ten sons?"* (1:8)

❖ Father, help me to see all the good things you have given me, especially my marriage. Don't let me destroy it, devaluing it because we have no children. Help me be a loving spouse and create a home where you can be present. Show me how to comfort my spouse so he or she does not feel judged by my disappointment. Help us to be happy together, and open to those you want to make part of our lives. I pray especially for (name your intention)

Our Father - Hail Mary - Glory Be

Fifth Day: *In the bitterness of her soul she prayed to the Lord and made a vow* (1:10)

❖ Lord, don't let me try to bargain with you or attempt to buy your favour. If I try to force you to do my will, it can only lead me to bitterness. Open my heart to see that your will is what can bring me true happiness. I pray especially for (name your intention)

Our Father - Hail Mary - Glory Be

Sixth Day: *[Eli] therefore supposed that she was drunk and said to her, "How long are you going to be in this drunken state? Rid yourself of your wine." (1:14)*

❖ Father, you know how I suffer because people think we have chosen not to have children. Sometimes they make careless jokes, not thinking how they hurt us. Help me not to become angry with them even if I don't show it. Help me not to strike back, but to be humble and (if it's appropriate) to ask them to pray for us. And help me to pray for them. I pray especially for (name your intention)

Our Father - Hail Mary - Glory Be

Seventh Day: *And with that the woman went away; she returned to the hall and ate and was dejected no longer. (1:18)*

❖ Father, I know you will answer my prayer in the way and at the time you choose. Give me the grace to recognise your answer. I know you will give me what is best for me because you love me. You will give me children in some way. If they are not the children of my body, perhaps they will be adopted, or children in some other way. Let me allow this to make me happy. Let me be open to your will and not cling on to the only answer I want. I pray especially for (name your intention)

Our Father - Hail Mary - Glory Be

Eighth Day: *This is the child I prayed for and the Lord granted me what I asked him. Now I make him over to the Lord for the whole of his life.* (1:27)

❖ However you give me children, Lord, don't allow me to make an idol of them. You don't give them to me so that I can fulfil myself and my dreams, but for me to bring them to you. Grant me wisdom and discernment in bringing them up, and grant them faith and the knowledge of your love for them. I pray especially for (name your intention)

Our Father - Hail Mary - Glory Be

Ninth Day: *My heart exults in the Lord, my horn is exalted in my God, my mouth derides my foes, for I rejoice in your power of saving.* (2:1)

❖ Father, I trust you. Give me the grace of an open heart. Give me the gift of joy. Let the Child Jesus be the first child born in me. Then, whatever my life is like, I will have the peace only you can give. I pray especially for (name your intention)

Our Father - Hail Mary - Glory Be

JOSEPH & HIS BROTHERS - FOR PEACE IN THE FAMILY

Scripture: *read the story of Joseph (Genesis 37-50)*

Joseph is one of twelve brothers. He is his father's favourite, and his brothers are jealous of him; he also has prophetic dreams, which sound to them like boasting. They plan to kill him, but at instead the last minute he is sold into slavery in Egypt. But his masters find him invaluable, and he rises to be adviser to Pharoah himself. This means he is able to give his brothers food when famine comes; and their reconciliation brings safety to the whole people of Israel.

First Day: *Israel loved Joseph more than his other sons, for he was the son of his old age…But his brothers, seeing how his father loved him more than all his other sons, came to hate him so much that they could not say a civil word to him.* (37:3-4)

This is a very familiar scene. We are very quick to detect slights, injustice, or favouritism from our earliest days; small children soon learn to say "but it's not fair!"

❖ Father, whatever the feelings of my heart, help me not to favour one of my children so as to be unjust to the others. Help me to know how to bring peace. I pray especially for (name your intention)

Our Father - Hail Mary - Glory Be

Second Day: *Now Joseph had a dream, and he repeated it to his brothers…" "We were binding sheaves in the countryside; and my sheaf, it seemed, rose up and stood upright; then I saw your sheaves gather round and bow to my sheaf." "So you want to be king over us," his brothers retorted"* (37:4-8)

Maybe Joseph told his dream in all innocence, not realising how it would seem to his brothers; but this was not how it was taken by them. Miscommunication and cross purposes can wreak havoc in family relationships; this danger today is made stronger by myriad means of communication, many of which, unlike old-fashioned conversation, make no allowance for tone of voice or context.

❖ Help us not to misinterpret each other, or read more into statements (or into silence) than is meant. Help us to hear each other charitably; and not to rush to judgement. I pray especially for (name your intention)

Our Father - Hail Mary - Glory Be

Third Day: *He had another dream..."I thought I saw the sun, the moon and eleven stars, bowing to me"...His father scolded him. "A fine dream to have!" he said to him. "Are all of us then, myself, your mother and your brothers, to come and bow to the ground before you?"* (37:9-10)

An unselfconscious, maybe precocious, child, or a bright and talkative young adult, may give offence without meaning it. We can recognise how annoying Joseph's talk must have been to his elders.

❖ Help us not to envy the different talents we see in others; help us, too, not to boast of what we have been given, or act or speak to put others down. Help us to trust that your plan for us is better than any plan we could devise. I pray especially for (name your intention)

Our Father - Hail Mary - Glory Be

Fourth day: *They made a plot among themselves to put him to death. "Here comes the man of dreams" they said to one another. "Come on, let us kill him and throw him into some well; we can say that a wild beast devoured him. Then we shall see what becomes of his dreams."* (37:18-20)

Anyone who has ever looked after small children will know that violent rage can sit easily alongside love for a brother or sister; and these hatreds and jealousies can be carried into later life. As we grow older, this is usually not as openly expressed, but is just as real; and, paradoxically, is less easy to be reconciled where the violence is all unexpressed or under the surface.

❖ Father, help me to acknowledge my anger, and I ask you to turn it aside. I pray especially for (name your intention)

Our Father - Hail Mary - Glory Be

Fifth Day: *But Reuben heard, and he saved him from their violence… "Shed no blood," said Reuben to them "throw him into this well in the wilderness, but do not lay violent hands on him" - intending to save him from them and restore him to his father.* (37:21-22)

Although Reuben had, presumably, been as angry as the other brothers about Joseph's apparent presumption and airs, he drew back from violence, and persuaded his brothers to agree.

❖ Father, help us not to cling to plans or feelings born out of anger; help us to be merciful to each other. I pray especially for (name your intention)

Our Father - Hail Mary - Glory Be

Sixth Day: *Now some Midianite merchants were passing, and they drew Joseph up out of the well. They sold Joseph to the Ishmaelites for twenty silver pieces, and these men took Joseph to Egypt. When Reuben went back to the well there was no sign of Joseph. Tearing his clothes, he went back to* *his brothers. "The boy has disappeared" he said. "What am I going to do?"* (37:28-30)

Reuben and the brothers are stricken with remorse and panic after their plan seems to have gone wrong, and had terrible consequences they had not intended.

❖ Father, help me to see that others may not have meant this situation to develop as it has; help us all not to blame each other for what may not be anyone's fault. I pray especially for (name your intention)

Our Father - Hail Mary - Glory Be

Seventh Day: *Joseph gave this order to his chamberlain: "Fill these men's sacks with as much food as they can carry, and put each man's money in the mouth of his sack. And put my cup, the silver one, in the mouth of the youngest one's sack"… When morning came and it was light, the men were sent off… They had scarcely left the city… before Joseph said to his chamberlain, "Away now and follow those men. When you catch up with them say to them, 'Why did you reward good with evil?'"* (44:1-4)

Joseph, now a high official in Egypt, uses a series of tricks and ruses to deceive and humiliate his brothers before he makes himself known to them.

Father, help me not to take pleasure in being right, or use whatever wrong has been done me as an excuse to revenge myself or humiliate others. I pray especially for (name your intention)

Our Father - Hail Mary - Glory Be

Eighth Day: *So ten of Joseph's brothers went down to buy grain in Egypt…It was Joseph, as the man in authority over the country, who sold the grain to all comers. So Joseph's brothers went and bowed low before him, their faces touching the ground. …So Joseph recognised his brothers, but they did not recognise him.* (42:3, 6, 8)

The brothers are able to accept and respect Joseph because they do not know it is him. Often we are so bound by our long habits of seeing and relating to a brother, or sister, or parent that we cannot make a fair appraisal of their qualities. Only, perhaps, if we can see them without prejudice (as if they were a stranger) can we see what may be obvious to others. God, thankfully, sees us all without prejudice.

❖ Father, help me to see with your eyes, unclouded by the hurts and confusions of the past. I pray especially for (name your intention)

Our Father - Hail Mary - Glory Be

Ninth Day: *I am your brother Joseph whom you sold into Egypt. But now, do not grieve, do not reproach yourselves for having sold me here, since God sent me before you to preserve your lives.* (45:4-5)

If God grants us reconciliation, we must pray not to dwell overmuch on whatever has now been resolved and forgiven: God takes our mistakes and sins and turns them to a good end we could not have foreseen. This is what we mean by providence.

❖ Father, let us know hope and the joy of renewal, not fruitless regret for a past that cannot be changed, but from which you can bring some new thing. I pray especially for (name your intention)

Our Father - Hail Mary - Glory Be

David & Absalom
and the Prodigal Son
- estranged children

Scripture: *read the story of David and Absalom*
(*2 Samuel* 13:1-19:4)

David, King of Israel, had many wives and many children and there was quite a competition between them. Absalom was his third son, handsome and admired. He had a beautiful sister called Tamar, who was raped by their half brother Amnon. David heard of this; but although he was angry, he did nothing because Amnon was his eldest son and had first place in his heart. So Absalom took matters into his own hands, and had Amnon murdered. David first exiled Absalom, but then forgave him, without, however, addressing any of the deeper questions involved. Absalom now despised his father and decided to take his throne. War broke out between them. Absalom was killed after getting his head caught in a tree and being discovered helpless by David's army. David mourned for his son.

Scripture: *read the story of the Prodigal Son*
(*Luke* 15:11-32)

The Prodigal Son is the younger of two sons. His father intends to divide everything equally between his two sons when he dies but the younger son does not want to wait. He does not want to be beholden to his father but wants the money as his right. As soon as he gets the money he leaves home, goes far away and lives a life of debauchery. This doesn't work out for him, so he plans what he can say to get his father to take him back. But as soon as he comes back, his father runs out to meet him and celebrates his return. The elder brother is angry, but the father is not dissuaded. He takes nothing away from the elder, while he is glad the younger has returned.

First Day: *My son Absalom! Absalom, my son, my son!*
(*2 S* 19:5)

Despite his wanting to destroy him, David still loved Absalom, and when he died he was grief stricken.

❖ Father, you know that despite all that has happened between us, I still love my child. I suffer because I see him (her) suffer, and I really want us to be reconciled. Give me hope that this will happen. I pray especially for (name your intention)

Our Father - Hail Mary - Glory Be

Second Day: *When David heard the whole story, he was very angry; but he had no wish to harm his son Amnon, since he loved him; he was his first born. (2 S 13:21)*

Absalom felt his father David didn't deal with injustice, so he took matters into his own hands.

❖ Lord, open my eyes to see the times I didn't act for the best; when I was unjust and offended my son (daughter); when I treated them differently. If it is right, then let me find a way to ask their forgiveness for that. Help me also to deal with any events my son (daughter) has misunderstood or misinterpreted. I pray especially for (name your intention)

Our Father - Hail Mary - Glory Be

Third Day: *Absalom sent couriers throughout the tribes of Israel saying, "When you hear the trumpet sound you are to say, 'Absalom is king at Hebron!'" (2 S 15:10)*

Although we may think David had given Absalom some cause to be resentful, nothing that happened could justify him in raising rebellion against his father. Absalom made a series of deliberate decisions to do what he knew was wrong.

❖ Lord, I know my child is an adult so their bad choices are their responsibility. Don't let me uselessly blame myself - or worse, blame my spouse - for all that has happened. I can only pray for my son (daughter) and hope for his (her) return to the Church and to the family. Help me to leave the judgement of the past to you. I pray especially for (name your intention)

Our Father - Hail Mary - Glory Be

Fourth Day: *Absalom...had taken flight and gone...he stayed for three years. And all that time the king mourned for his son. (2 S 13:37-8)*

After Absalom had Amnon killed, David sent him into exile, and didn't let him come back for a while. In doing this, he was thinking of the rest of his family.

❖ Father, give me wisdom in this situation. Help me remember that the whole family is involved and all of us must be heard. Let me (us) not gain my lost child at the expense of his (her) brother (sister). Our reconciliation must be honest. I pray especially for (name your intention)

Our Father - Hail Mary - Glory Be

Fifth Day: *So the father divided his property between them. A few days later, the younger son got together everything he had and left for a distant country where he squandered his money on a life of debauchery. (Lk 15:12-13)*

The younger son ("the prodigal") went far away, and did his own thing, living in a way very different to all he had been taught or had known.

❖ Lord, you know how hurt I am that my son (daughter) seems to have rejected everything we taught him (her); how hurt I am by his (her) wish to have nothing to do with us. Strengthen me (us) and let me (us) not lose confidence in my (our) abilities as parents to all my (our) children. I pray especially for (name your intention)

Our Father - Hail Mary - Glory Be

Sixth Day: *When he had spent it all, that country experienced a severe famine, and now he began to feel the pinch…Then he came to his senses (Lk 15:14, 17)*

The younger son suffered, but that suffering brought him back.

❖ I see that my son (daughter) suffers in the life he (she) has chosen, but I know that you can bring good out of even the worst situation. Free him (her) from his (her) poor choices and may his (her) situation spur him (her) to return to you and to us. I pray especially for (name your intention)

Our Father - Hail Mary - Glory Be

Seventh Day: *Then he came to his senses and said, "How many of my father's paid servants have more food than they want, and here am I dying of hunger! I will…go to my father and say: Father, I have sinned…" (Lk 15:17-18)*

The younger son makes a cynical calculation about his situation; he is hardly truly repentant. But even though he wasn't sincere, his father welcomed him.

❖ Father, give me an open heart, ready to forgive if asked. Help me to push aside the rancour and blame and try to make a new beginning. I pray especially for (name your intention)

Our Father - Hail Mary - Glory Be

Eighth Day: *The elder son...was angry then and refused to go in, and his father came out to plead with him; but he answered his father, "Look, all these years I have slaved for you and never once disobeyed your orders, yet you never offered me so much as a kid for me to celebrate with my friends..." (Lk 15:28-29)*

The elder brother is angry, but his father took nothing away from him.

❖ Father, help me to broker peace with the rest of the family. May they not feel less loved because their sibling has returned. Let them not believe that we are less soft-hearted with them. They have stayed close to us. Let them see we value their loyalty and restraint. I pray especially for (name your intention)

Our Father - Hail Mary - Glory Be

Ninth Day: *My son, you are with me always and all I have is yours. But it was only right we should celebrate and rejoice, because your brother here was dead and has come to life; he was lost and is found.* (Lk 15:31-32)

God's mercy is not limited, and does not exclude anyone; we too have been often in need of his mercy and compassion, and will be so again.

Finally, Lord, help me remember how many times you have forgiven me. Give me a grateful heart, and help me to show to others the mercy I have received. I pray especially for (name your intention)

Our Father - Hail Mary - Glory Be

MARTHA - BEING THE ONE THAT DOES ALL THE WORK

Scripture: *read the story of Martha*
(*Luke* 10:38-42 and *John* 11:1-54)

 In Jesus's life on earth, he lived as we do. He had family, and he also had friends. Amongst his friends were two sisters and a brother, Martha, Mary, and Lazarus. They lived in a village called Bethany, and Jesus often visited them there.

First Day: *A woman named Martha welcomed him into her house.* (*Lk* 10:38)

Martha lived with her brother and sister, but Luke says that she was the one in charge of the house. She was capable and organised and it was she who took charge when Jesus visited them.

❖ Lord, I thank you that you have given me the capabilities I have. I ask you to accept them as a gift from you without selfish pride, but without false modesty either. Please give me also the gifts of hospitality and service so that I can use my talents as you planned. I pray especially for (name your intention)

Our Father - Hail Mary - Glory Be

Second Day: *Martha...was distracted with all the serving* (*Lk* 10:40)

Martha wanted everything to be done well, but she got so caught up in this that she missed the point of the visit.

❖ Don't let me be so keen to have things perfect that I make everything uncomfortable for everyone, and embarrass and depress the people I am supposed to be helping. Let me do what I can to the best of my abilities, but not worry about the things I can't achieve. I pray especially for (name your intention)

Our Father - Hail Mary - Glory Be

Third Day: *Lord, do you not care that my sister is leaving me to do the serving all by myself?* (*Lk* 10:40)

Martha was doing all that was needed for her visitors' comfort and her sister was not helping her, but had joined the men and was listening to Jesus.

❖ Lord, I feel that I am left to do all the work, and people who could help me just don't do anything. Help me not to be angry with them. Have I made it difficult for them to help because of my impatience, or by insisting on doing things a particular way? Don't allow me to judge you either, or believe you do not care about me. Give me the grace to be at peace, knowing I am working in your service, and to leave the rest to you. You can take away the feeling I have of being burdened, if I give it over to you whose yoke is light. I pray especially for (name your intention)

Our Father - Hail Mary - Glory Be

Fourth Day: *But the Lord answered…"Mary has chosen the better part; it is not to be taken from her." (Lk 10:41-42)*

Martha hoped Jesus would tell Mary to help her - it was only fair - but he didn't. Instead, he told her she was wrong and Mary was right.

❖ Lord, sometimes it's hard that others don't seem to see how I am taken advantage of and put upon. Nobody seems to think of me. They don't encourage others to help me; they seem to think I will just get on with things. Help me not to be resentful and full of judgement. Give me the wisdom to see the good in other people, and the good other people do. I pray especially for (name your intention)

Our Father - Hail Mary - Glory Be

Fifth Day: *You worry and fret about so many things, and yet few are needed, indeed only one. (Lk 10:41-42)*

Martha expected Jesus's support in her anger with her sister, but instead he gently rebuked her.

❖ Help me to see where your rebukes are in my life. Help me to see my life as you do; to see my own faults, not the faults of others; but also to know you love me in spite of my faults, and you are with me every day. I pray especially for (name your intention)

Our Father - Hail Mary - Glory Be

Sixth Day: *When Martha heard Jesus had come she went out to meet him (Jn 11:20)*

When Jesus called her, Martha went out to meet him. She was not trapped in her routines or her small world of work. He called, and she went.

❖ Lord, let me know how much you love me; how exciting life with you can be. Give me the gift of joy. I am tempted to turn in on myself, to harden my heart; but with your help I can be open to the life you give me. If I know you are with me, I can even be happy. I pray especially for (name your intention)

Our Father - Hail Mary - Glory Be

Seventh Day: *I know that whatever you ask of God he will grant you (Jn 11:22)*

Martha is one of the first to realise Jesus is the Christ.

❖ Lord, give me the grace to see you, to know you, and to know you have power to help me. Let me see you are helping me: helping me in my situation in life; helping me grow in faith. Give me the trust in you that Martha had. I pray especially for (name your intention)

Our Father - Hail Mary - Glory Be

Eighth Day: *Jesus wept* (*Jn* 11:35)

When Martha's brother died, Jesus wept, even though he was going to raise him from the dead. He wept because he loved them.

❖ Lord, I know you love me too, and that you weep over me; not only for my sins but for my sufferings. May I feel the comfort of your closeness. May I be strengthened by the certainty you love me. I pray especially for (name your intention)

Our Father - Hail Mary - Glory Be

Ninth Day: *Go, therefore, make disciples of all the nations* (*Mt* 28:19)

Tradition says that, after Pentecost, Martha went with her brother and sister to announce the Gospel in Tarascon in France, and that she either destroyed a dragon or turned people away from worshipping one.

❖ Lord, I ask you to give me hope. Let me see that the difficulties I have do not define my life. You have great plans for me if I walk with you. Even if my physical circumstances don't change, if I stay close to you, I can do great things in your eyes. I pray especially for (name your intention)

Our Father - Hail Mary - Glory Be

Ruth and Naomi - feeling abandoned and forgotten

Scripture: *read the Book of Ruth*

There was a famine in Israel, so Naomi's husband sold his land and took his family to Moab. Soon afterwards, he died, leaving Naomi stranded there. Her two sons married Moabite women, but after some time the sons too died. Having nothing in either country, Naomi decided to return to Israel. One of her two daughters-in-law stayed in Moab, but the other, Ruth, did not want to leave the elderly Naomi to fend for herself and vowed to stay with her and live how and where Naomi did. The two women returned to Israel and Ruth worked to support them in a menial and even dangerous job. Naomi used her wisdom to find Ruth a husband. The love between mother-in-law and daughter-in-law may not be the first thing we think of when we talk about human love, but in this case, and in many others, it is a strong sign of God's acting in spite of human prejudice and limitations.

First Day: *A man called Elimelech, his wife Naomi, and his two sons, Mahlon and Chillon…came to the country of Moab and settled there. Elimelech, Naomi's husband died… then Mahlon and Chillon also died and the woman was bereft of her two sons and her husband.* (1:2-3, 5)

Naomi was in a foreign country where she had been taken by her husband.

❖ Father, I feel so alone. I feel there is nobody to support and love me, and nobody for me to love. I am isolated from others and have nothing in common with people. Help me not to let this feeling overwhelm and destroy me. Don't let me blame others for my situation. Help me to lean on you. I know you can pull me out of this pit. I pray especially for (name your intention)

Our Father - Hail Mary - Glory Be

Second Day: *The women said, "Can this be Naomi?" But she said to them, "Do not call me Naomi, call me Mara, for Shaddai has marred me bitterly. Filled full I departed, the Lord brings me back empty."* (1:19-21)

My life seems such a failure. I hoped it would be so different. I see other people who seem to have everything I want and I feel so bitter. Why have you forgotten me? And yet Ruth chose you and everything she had lost was restored to her and more.

❖ Kindle a flame of hope in me. Give me a grateful heart because I know you. Give me hope that you can enter my loneliness and comfort me. Help me to see my life as you see it: not its failures and disappointments, but what it can be, so that I too can be a sign of faith in you. I pray especially for (name your intention)

Our Father - Hail Mary - Glory Be

Third Day: *Ruth said, "…wherever you go, I will go, wherever you live, I will live. Your people shall be my people and your God, my God." (1:16)*

Ruth chose God and stuck to her choice. Ruth chose to stay with Naomi rather than remaining with her own people with a chance of marrying again. This beautiful expression of love is not between spouses but between a mother- and daughter-in-law. Help me see the love that is in my life and to value it, even if it is not the kind of love I long for. I pray especially for (name your intention)

Our Father - Hail Mary - Glory Be

Fourth Day: *Ruth the Moabitess said to Naomi, "Let me go into the fields and glean among the ears of corn". (2:1)*

❖ Father, show me that work is valuable in itself. It doesn't have to be high status. All work can have dignity and all work is done for your glory. Also caring for others is not meant to be a burden. Help me to see that in loving my dependents I make it possible for you to act in my life. I pray especially for (name your intention)

Our Father - Hail Mary - Glory Be

Fifth Day: *Boaz said to Ruth, "Listen... You are not to glean in any other field, do not leave here but stay with my servants... And if you are thirsty, go to the pitchers and drink..." And she said to him, "How have I so earned your favour?" And Boaz answered her, "I have been told all you have done for your mother-in-law since your husband's death...May the Lord reward you for what you have done!" (2:8-12)*

Boaz was kind to a foreigner, someone with no status or influence, and she became his wife.

❖ Help me to be open and kind. Give me concern for the weak and show me the way I can be some help, no matter in how small a way. I pray especially for (name your intention)

Our Father - Hail Mary - Glory Be

Sixth Day: *Then Naomi said to her, "Now tonight [Boaz] is winnowing the barley at the threshing-floor. Come, wash and anoint and dress yourself. Then go down to the threshing-floor." (3:1-3)*

❖ Father, help me not to become careless of my appearance and hygiene because I think my life worthless. I am not a person nobody cares for. I am deeply loved by you. I pray especially for (name your intention)

Our Father - Hail Mary - Glory Be

Seventh Day: *"A son has been born for Naomi" they said; and they named him Obed. This was the father of David's father, Jesse.* (4:17)

No one is unimportant in the fulfilment of God's plan - each of us has a part. Naomi was old and Ruth a foreigner; both were women alone in a male dominated world, but between them they allowed God's plan to progress. Ruth married Boaz and gave birth to Obed, who was the grandfather of King David and thus an ancestor of Jesus Christ.

❖ Father, you can do great things with me too. You can give me my heart's desire, but whatever my life is, I know that you can give me happiness if I allow you to. Nothing is wasted in your sight. I pray especially for (name your intention)

Our Father - Hail Mary - Glory Be

Eighth Day: *So Boaz took Ruth and she became his wife. And when they came together, the Lord made her conceive and she bore a son. And the women said to Naomi, "Blessed be the Lord who has not left the dead man without next of kin this day to perpetuate his name in Israel. The child will* *be a comfort to you and the prop of your old age, for your daughter-in-law who loves you and is more to you than seven sons has given him birth."* (4:14-16)

God can bring life out of death. When Ruth's son was born, he was counted as the son of her first husband and he was brought up by Naomi.

❖ I see you can give life and fruitfulness to the old and the dead, and you can give me this too. I pray especially for (name your intention)

Our Father - Hail Mary - Glory Be

Ninth Day: *Seeing his mother and the disciple he loved standing near her, Jesus said to his mother "Woman, this is your son." Then to the disciple he said, "This is your mother."* (*Jn* 19:26-27)

Naomi is reckoned as a *type* of the Virgin Mary. She helped Ruth to find a husband and a home; to find the place God had prepared for her.

❖ I ask you, Mary, to be my mother, to guide my life; to bring me to your son; to help me learn to love and be happy. I pray especially for (name your intention)

Our Father - Hail Mary - Glory Be

DEBORAH AND BARAK - WHEN
THINGS SEEM TOO MUCH FOR US

Scripture: *read the story of Deborah and Barak (Judges 4-5)*

After they entered the Promised Land, the people of Israel were at first ruled by judges, chosen by God. The Israelites were surrounded by pagan nations and war was commonplace. The story of Deborah and Barak shows how God works through unexpected means and individuals to protect Israel, his chosen people.

First Day: *At this time Deborah was a judge in Israel, a prophetess, the wife of Lappidoth.* (4:4)

Deborah was the only female judge of Israel (out of twelve) and lived at a time when women were secondary to men. She combined this heavy responsibility with domestic responsibilities. She was able to do this because she depended on God

❖ Father, I ask for your reassurance that I can live my responsibilities together with you. Even though I feel overwhelmed by what I have to do, by those I have to care for, by all the things I have to juggle, I know that you are with me. Even if I sometimes fail, I can be at peace, knowing you love me and those who depend on me, and that you will not abandon us. I pray especially for (name your intention)

Our Father - Hail Mary - Glory Be

Second Day: *She sent for Barak…She said to him, "This is the order of the Lord, the God of Israel…"* (4:6)

Barak was the person chosen by God to lead his armies, but he had to be called from far away to come and do his duty. Some Jewish rabbis say Barak is actually Deborah's husband Lappidoth. This is because Lappidoth means "torchlight" and Barak means "lightning". Before this battle he was like a small light but Deborah called him to become like lightning.

❖ Lord, help me not to judge others who should share my burdens but who I feel are failing to do so, leaving everything to me. Let me lean on you instead of crushing them with my demands and my contempt. Give me the right way to encourage them, and give them the confidence they need to help deal with the difficulties we face. I pray especially for (name your intention)

Our Father - Hail Mary - Glory Be

Third Day: *Barak answered her, "If you come with me, I will go; if you will not come, I will not go, for I do not know how to choose the day when the Lord will grant me success".* (4:8)

Barak is willing to go, but admits he does not have Deborah's faith. Deborah chides him for his lack of trust in God but marches with him as he leads the men into battle.

❖ Father, help me remember I have to work with others. If I lean on you, I can support them, even if they have to lean on me. Show me how to treat them with respect. Help me not to get impatient when they do things more slowly than I want, or not in the way I want. Don't let me despise and reject their help, or leave them behind and try to do everything alone. If they refuse to help me, I still have your help, but let me always respect them and be ready to accept their help. I pray especially for (name your intention)

Our Father - Hail Mary - Glory Be

Fourth Day: *Once again the Israelites began to do what displeases the Lord, and the Lord handed them over to Jabin the king of Canaan...The commander of his army was Sisera* (4:1-2)

The Israelites were chosen to live a godly life, but instead they often tried to live like everyone else, focusing on their own wishes and not considering what was right. God uses the consequences of this to remind them he is there, waiting to help them.

❖ Lord, enlighten me about my own sins, about what I have done to make this situation worse - where my suffering is made worse because I don't trust you. I can't accept my weakness, and I don't accept the help of others for what it is. Give me the courage to pass this burden to you. Help me learn to walk with you. I pray especially for (name your intention)

Our Father - Hail Mary - Glory Be

Fifth Day: *Sisera…called for all his chariots - nine hundred chariots plated with iron - and all the troops he had.* (4:12-13)

Sisera was the commander of an immense enemy army, and once Barak went out to face them things appeared to get even worse. Sisera seemed an unbeatable foe.

❖ When I face up to my problems and responsibilities, help me not panic even if things are worse than I feared. Keep me close to you and to the sacraments, to give me the strength and discernment I need to carry on. I pray especially for (name your intention)

Our Father - Hail Mary - Glory Be

Sixth Day: *Deborah said to Barak, "Up! For today is the day the Lord has put Sisera into your power."* (4:14)

There was a moment when Barak had to act. He had to be ready, and act as Deborah told him. Barak was prepared and he was able to follow the orders of a woman at a time when that was almost unknown.

❖ May I never despair, never believe that nothing can be resolved. I know that even if the exterior situation does not change, with your help everything can change for me. Help me to recognise your voice and your hand in my life. Give me the humility to accept advice and the wisdom to know when to act on it. I pray especially for (name your intention)

Our Father - Hail Mary - Glory Be

Seventh Day: *Sisera meanwhile fled on foot towards the tent of Jael, the wife of Heber the Kenite…But Jael….took a tent peg and picked up a mallet; she crept up softly to him and drove the peg into his temple right through to the ground.* (4:17, 21)

When Sisera was routed in battle he fled to Heber, whom he counted as an ally, and asked help from Heber's wife. He thought he was safe; Heber's wife Jael was not was not someone he took any account of. But Jael was both wily and courageous. She lulled Sisera to sleep and then killed him.

❖ I understand that the enemy I have to kill is the Evil One. Give me the wisdom to see his lies and give me the courage to turn away from them. I may be weak and disregarded, but with you I am strong. Show me the truth of my life and give me the gift of joy even in suffering. I pray especially for (name your intention)

Our Father - Hail Mary - Glory Be

Eighth Day: *Barak…went into her tent; Sisera lay dead.* (4:22)

Deborah had prophesied that the glory would not be Barak's, but that Sisera would be delivered into the hand of a woman. Nor was that woman Deborah, the judge and prophetess, but Jael, who was "only a housewife".

❖ Show me that help can come from the most unexpected places, even from someone I haven't thought about. If you choose to resolve my situation without me, without warning, give me a grateful heart and help me not to doubt, but to trust that the situation is resolved. I pray especially for (name your intention)

Our Father - Hail Mary - Glory Be

Ninth Day: *And let those who love you be like the sun when he arises in all his strength.* (5:31)

❖ Help me to let go of my problems when you have solved them, and not to hold on to the suffering. Let me let go of my burdens when you carry them for me and not try to grab them back. Help me to know that my sufferings and my problems are not my identity. I pray especially for (name your intention)

Our Father - Hail Mary - Glory Be

Jonah - when God's plan doesn't seem to make sense

Scripture: *read the Book of Jonah*

Jonah is the story of a reluctant prophet; the story of a man who runs away from what he knows God is asking him to do, because (in his well-informed opinion) what God is suggesting is preposterous. God wants Jonah to go to the great city of Nineveh, a vast metropolis, and, on his own, tell them to turn from wickedness, or they will perish. It is an obviously absurd mission, and Jonah is properly dismissive of it. God however will not be put off, and uses various devices (storms, sea-monsters) that we may also think ridiculous or undignified to bring Jonah back to where he wants him. God means Jonah to be the one to save the people of Nineveh from themselves; and despite his own sense of outraged dignity, Jonah eventually sees that God is right.

First Day: *The word of the Lord was addressed to Jonah son of Amittai: "Up!" he said. "Go to Nineveh, the great city, and inform them that their wickedness has become known* *to me." Jonah decided to run away from the Lord, and go to Tarshish.* (1:1-3)

Jonah heard God clearly telling him to call the people of Nineveh to convert, but he refused to obey and went off in totally the opposite direction. This was not because he was unsure about what he should do, but because he really didn't want to do it. He put a lot of effort and some money into doing the opposite of the mission God called him to.

❖ Lord, you know there are issues in my life where I know what I should do as a Christian but it doesn't seem reasonable. Forgive me for the times I have not spoken due to fear or self-preservation; where I have not wanted to make myself vulnerable or open to ridicule. Have mercy on me for the times I have only been concerned with worldly things. I pray especially for (name your intention)

Our Father - Hail Mary - Glory Be

Second Day: *The Lord unleashed a violent wind on the sea, and there was such a great storm…that the ship threatened to break up…The sailors rowed hard in an effort to reach the shore, but in vain…They then called on the Lord and said "O Lord, do not let us perish for taking this man's life…"* (1:4, 13-14)

The pagans pray and sacrifice, give up their goods and try everything to save everyone, even Jonah although they know he is to blame. The sailors didn't have the gift of faith, but they were kind. They also asked God not to blame them.

❖ Lord, help me not to look down on those who do not know you. I pray especially for (name your intention)

Our Father - Hail Mary - Glory Be

Third Day: *The sailors took fright, and each of them called on his own god, and to lighten the ship they threw the cargo overboard. Jonah, however, had gone below and lain down in the hold and fallen fast asleep. (1:5)*

When the storm threatened the ship, all the pagans prayed and sacrificed, but Jonah, who was supposed to be a friend of God's, only slept.

❖ There are times I have not acted, have not asked your help, have made no effort to protest about laws or actions that are against your laws. Forgive me for my apathy, for thinking first of my comfort. Forgive me for feeling indifferent, not responsible or even smug, and leaving people in their sin. I pray especially for (name your intention)

Our Father - Hail Mary - Glory Be

Fourth Day: *The sailors were seized with terror...and said "What have you done?" They then said, "What are we to do with you?"...He replied, "Take me and throw me into the sea...for I can see it is my fault this violent storm has* *happened to you."…And taking hold of Jonah they threw him into the sea; and the sea grew calm again.* (1:10-12, 15)

Jonah understands why the storm is raging, and knows that the only way to save the others is for him to be thrown overboard. He offers this, and persuades the others to do it. The sea is immediately calm and the ship is saved because of Jonah's sacrifice. The sailors see what happens and are converted.

❖ Lord, you know that giving up your life for others seems like insanity or only the job of a few saints. Even if in my mind I know this is the mission of all Christians, it still seems ridiculous. Show me what "giving up my life" means in my life, and give me the desire for your spirit to fulfil this in me. Help me to do this without fear, knowing you love me. I pray especially for (name your intention)

Our Father - Hail Mary - Glory Be

Fifth Day: *The Lord had arranged that a great fish should be there to swallow Jonah* (2:1)

When Jonah was thrown overboard into a raging sea, he did not drown as anyone would expect, but he was swallowed by a large fish.

❖ Lord, give me faith to know that if I risk on you, if I do the right thing, you will protect me, even if the next thing that happens doesn't seem so perfect either. May I see that we are moving forward together and I can rest in your will. I pray especially for (name your intention)

Our Father - Hail Mary - Glory Be

Sixth Day: *Jonah remained in the belly of the fish for three days and three nights.* (2:1)

Jonah found himself trapped in the belly of a large fish. He was literally in the dark. He couldn't control anything; he had to go where the fish was going. He had to trust that God was in control. Finally, he found himself in the place God wanted him to be without his having made any effort to get there.

❖ Lord, help me to be at peace if there are times in my life when I can't move, I can't see where to go and I find myself helpless in a situation I did not choose. Help me to believe that you are in charge of everything that happens, and that my life is moving towards where you want it to be. I pray especially for (name your intention)

Our Father - Hail Mary - Glory Be

Seventh Day: *From the belly of the fish he prayed to the Lord, his God; and he said, "Out of my distress I cried to the Lord and he answered me"* (2:2-3)

Jonah understood that God had saved him, and began a prayer of thanks even though his situation was not immediately obviously safe. He uses the Psalms to pray.

❖ I ask for the grace to be able to see my life as you see it, to see where you have pulled me out of danger and to believe that you protect me even if I can't see it. Remind me to turn to you in the Scriptures. I pray especially for (name your intention)

Our Father - Hail Mary - Glory Be

Eighth Day: *Jonah set out and went to Nineveh…he preached in these words, "Only forty days more and Nineveh is going to be destroyed." And the people of Nineveh believed in God… God saw their efforts to renounce their evil behaviour. And God relented…Jonah was very indignant at this; he fell into a rage.* (3:3, 4-5, 10; 4:1)

The large fish vomits Jonah out on the shore exactly where he was originally asked to go. Jonah calls the Ninevites to repentance, as he was asked to do, and the Ninevites repent. Jonah is furious. He knew that if he were really a prophet, this would happen; and now he is angry. He wants to be right in doubting God and he doesn't want the Ninevites to repent and be saved. It is far too easy. He feels they should suffer.

❖ You know that sometimes I feel people are given easy forgiveness, especially if they have done something against me. I don't want to forgive them and I don't want you to forgive them either. When you forgive my enemies, I feel that you don't take me seriously or the hurt that is done to me. Help me to see that you forgive me as lovingly as you forgive my enemies, and give me the desire to forgive as you do. I pray especially for (name your intention)

Our Father - Hail Mary - Glory Be

Ninth Day: *God said to Jonah..."Am I not to feel sorry for Nineveh, the great city, in which there are more than a hundred and twenty thousand people?"* (4:9-11)

The conversion of the Ninevites depends on God, not on Jonah. It would take three days to travel across Nineveh, let alone speak to all the inhabitants; but they convert after only one day of Jonah's preaching. God is quick to forgive those who recognise their faults and repent as the Ninevites do. He even sends Jonah to show them their faults. God pities them.

❖ Lord, give me the gift of a merciful heart and the courage and humility not to let my own sense of dignity or self-importance stand in the way of your love for me and for others; let me be able to believe in your mercy and forgiveness, even when it comes through apparently weak or unworthy or ridiculous people (such as myself). I pray especially for (name your intention)

Our Father - Hail Mary - Glory Be

JOB - BEING HONEST WITH GOD

Scripture: *read the Book of Job*

Job has always been an emblematic figure: brought low by a whim of God from happiness and prosperity to the depths of misery, his story is a showcase for the various ways people have tried to explain away human suffering. For Job, as for us, these efforts at explanation are mostly useless, where they are not actively annoying or enraging. Job, like us, is not soothed by simplistic reasonings; in the end, it is only the vision of God's transcendent majesty that allows him to move beyond his own misery. Like Job, we are unlikely to be helped by argument or advice, however well-intentioned, but by an encounter with the living God; and this is why we need to pray.

First Day: *"Stretch out your hand and lay a finger on his bone and flesh; I warrant you, he will curse you to your face." "Very well," the Lord said to Satan, "he is in your power."* (2:5-6)

God gives Job, a righteous and God-fearing man, into the power of the Enemy for the express purpose of testing his faith. He has done nothing wrong. What happens to him is deeply unfair. Yet Job does not blame God, although he does fall into deep despair.

❖ Father, sometimes what happens to me seems grossly unfair, and it seems as if you are punishing me without cause. Help me not to worry fruitlessly about how I may have offended you. Help me to believe you are my loving Father, however hard it may be to think so. I pray especially for (name your intention)

Our Father - Hail Mary - Glory Be

Second Day: *"If we take happiness from God's hand, must we not take sorrow too?" And in all this misfortune Job uttered no sinful word...In the end Job...cursed the day of his birth: "May the day perish when I was born..."* (2:10, 3:1-3)

At first, Job utters conventional sentiments of acceptance; his wife is not convinced by this, and, before long, she is proved right when he curses the day of his birth and sees only misery and unreason. His conventional defences are down; he is at rock bottom.

❖ Father, help me not to take refuge in simplistic pieties or a gritted teeth acceptance that does not admit the reality or the extent of my hurt, my sadness, my disappointment.

Help me not to hide from you behind rationalisations. I pray especially for (name your intention)

Our Father - Hail Mary - Glory Be

Third Day: *Is not man's life on earth nothing more than pressed service, his time no better than hired drudgery?... Lying in bed I wonder, "When will it be day?" Risen I think, "How slowly evening comes!"...Swifter than a weaver's shuttle my days have passed, and vanished, leaving no hope behind. Remember that my life is but a breath, and my eyes will never again see joy.* (7:1, 4, 6-7)

Job is honest in declaring his despair at the bleak sameness he experiences; day in, day out, he finds nothing to lift his spirits or suggest God cares about him. Until we uncover our true feelings, rather than whatever pretence or façade we may show to the world, or use to get us through the day, we cannot expect God to touch us.

❖ Father, help me to show you my true face, not the masks I put on for the world to see. I pray especially for (name your intention)

Our Father - Hail Mary - Glory Be

Fourth Day: *Since I have lost all taste for life, I will give free rein to my complaints; I shall let my embittered soul speak out. I shall say to God, "Do not condemn me, but tell me the reason for your assault. Is it right for you to injure me,*

78

cheapening the work of your own hands, and abetting the schemes of the wicked?...And if I make a stand, like a lion you hunt me down, adding to the tale of your triumphs". (10:1-3, 16)

Job cannot understand what has happened to him; his pain gives him honesty, and he is baffled by the apparent futility of God's doings. Why bother to make him, and pick him up when he falls, only to knock him down again?

❖ Father, I do not understand your ways with me. Sometimes I feel you only give me relief from my suffering to prepare me to have it again, and worse. Help me in my pain to find honesty, and tell you what I truly feel, not what I think you want me to say. I pray especially for (name your intention)

Our Father - Hail Mary - Glory Be

Fifth Day: *God has made my heart sink, Shaddai has filled me with fear. For darkness hides me from him, and the gloom veils his presence from me...Fatherless children are robbed of their lands, and poor men have their cloaks seized as security. From the towns come the groans of the dying and the gasp of wounded men crying for help. Yet God remains deaf to their appeal!* (23:16-17; 24:9, 12)

Job is filled with dread by what God seems to be like, if he is even there. Everywhere, evil triumphs, and the innocent and weak are oppressed without God lifting a finger to help them.

❖ Father, you know how terror and dismay are often my companions, and how sometimes I can see only sadness and futility. Help me to know you are there, even in darkness and pain. I pray especially for (name your intention)

Our Father - Hail Mary - Glory Be

Sixth Day: *Have I been insensible to poor men's needs, or let a widow's eyes grow dim?...Have I put all my trust in gold? Have I taken pleasure in my enemies' misfortunes, or made merry when disaster overtook them, I who allowed my tongue to do no wrong?...Have I ever hidden my sins from men, keeping my iniquity secret?...Who can get me a hearing from God?* (31:16, 24, 29-30, 33, 35)

Job speaks of his righteousness, not to boast, but to ask, "What is the point? Even I, who have done all this, who have been merciful, am afflicted."

❖ Father, let me not try to make bargains with you by doing good works; or think they are all worthless because I am suffering. Help me to be merciful. I pray especially for (name your intention)

Our Father - Hail Mary - Glory Be

Seventh Day: *Then from the heart of the tempest the Lord gave Job his answer. He said: "Where were you when I laid the earth's foundations? Tell me, since you are so well-informed! Who decided the dimensions of it, do you* *know? Or who stretched the measuring-line across it? What supports its pillars at their bases? Who laid its cornerstone when all the stars of the morning were singing with joy, and the Sons of God in chorus were chanting praise? Who pent up the sea behind closed doors when it leapt tumultuous out of the womb, when I wrapped it in a robe of mist and made black clouds its swaddling bands...have you journeyed all the way to the sources of the sea, or walked where the Abyss is deepest?"* (38:1, 4-9, 16-17)

God's first answer to Job does not address any of his arguments, but describes the myriad wonders of the created world, and asks, "Did you do this?" This may seem an empty answer; but simply looking at a spring sunrise may do more for our misery than a library of arguments.

❖ Father, help me not to close my eyes to all you have made. Help me to see there is more than I can know. I pray especially for (name your intention)

Our Father - Hail Mary - Glory Be

Eighth Day: *Now think of Behemoth...his bones are as hard as hammered iron. He is the masterpiece of God's work... Leviathan, too! Can you catch him with a fish-hook?...Who dare open the gates of his mouth? Terror dwells in those rows of teeth...His heart is as hard as rock, unyielding as a millstone. Sword may strike him, but it cannot pierce him... He churns the depths into a seething cauldron, he makes the* *sea fume like a scent burner…of all the sons of pride he is the king.* (40:15, 18-19, 25; 41:6, 16, 18, 23, 26)

God's second answer is a long description of two primeval monsters of chaos, taken from the old myths of the near east: Behemoth who stalks the land, and Leviathan, the great sea-dragon. Even these, God says, are of his making; he governs and restrains them, whom no man might even look on.

Father, help me to see that you are behind all things, even the most terrifying or appalling events, and that you walk with us, unseen. I pray especially for (name your intention)

Our Father - Hail Mary - Glory Be

Ninth Day: *This was the answer Job gave to the Lord: "I know that you are all-powerful: what you conceive, you can perform. I am the man who obscured your designs with my empty-headed words."…The Lord turned to Eliphaz. "I burn with anger against you" he said "for not speaking truthfully about me as my servant Job has done."* (42:1-3, 7)

God does not rebut any of Job's accusations, or make some long speech of theological apologetics. He is angry not with Job for his honesty, but with his friends who have tried to give easy answers. We may quote Richard Rohr: "When Jesus was looking down on Jerusalem and weeping over it (*Lk* 19:41) the last thing he needed was a pious man running up to him and saying, 'Now, Lord, don't cry. It's all part of God's perfect plan'. No, let Jesus weep. The bigger problem is that we do not join with him in weeping..."[5]

❖ Father, let me not run after easy answers, but take your words into my heart. Be close to me, this day and all days. I pray especially for (name your intention)

Our Father - Hail Mary - Glory Be

Abraham - old age

Scripture: *read the story of Abraham* (*Genesis* 12-25)

Abram, who becomes Abraham, is an old man, settled in his ways, and at a deep level a disappointed man: he has no children, no one to carry on his name and his family. Without warning, God calls him to leave all this behind, and makes him frankly unbelievable promises of future happiness. Abraham risks everything on answering God's call; and despite backsliding and occasional scepticism, he sees all God's promises fulfilled. The faith he is given allows him to trust God even when he asks him to sacrifice to him the very son and heir he had longed for.

First Day: *The Lord said to Abram, "Leave your country, your family and your father's house, for the land I will show you. I will make you a great nation; I will bless you and make your name so famous that it will be used as a blessing."…So Abram went as the Lord told him…Abram was seventy-five years old when he left Haran.* (12:1-2, 4)

God called Abraham when he was settled and old.

❖ Father, you call me too to the Promised Land. Every day is a step nearer to heaven to be with you. But, Father, teach me to hear your voice, to know that the journey is also important. Every day is also a new beginning. Let me always be expectant so that this does not pass me by. I pray especially for (name your intention)

Our Father - Hail Mary - Glory Be

Second Day: *Abram's wife Sarai had borne him no child, but she had an Egyptian maidservant named Hagar. So Sarai said to Abram, "Listen, now! Since the Lord has kept me from having children, go to my slave-girl. Perhaps I shall get children through her." Abram agreed to what Sarai had said...Hagar bore Abram a son.* (16:1-2, 15)

The incident of Hagar's son is a sign that Abraham has given up on God's promise to him, and is settling for second best.

❖ Help me not to be disappointed, not to think "is this all there is?" Let me see my life as you do. Help me see myself as a friend of yours. Teach me to accept with humility my failing capacities, and to rejoice that my growing weakness makes me more like you on the cross. I pray especially for (name your intention)

Our Father - Hail Mary - Glory Be

Third Day: *Abram took his wife Sarai, his nephew Lot, all the possessions they had amassed...They set off for the land of Canaan.* (12:5)

Although Abraham was old, and childless, he had a wife to share his life with.

❖ Let me not forget the good things of my life - not just the life I enjoyed when I was younger, but also the life I have now. I pray especially for (name your intention)

Our Father - Hail Mary - Glory Be

Fourth Day: *He looked up, and there he saw three men standing near him. As soon as he saw them he ran from the entrance of the tent to meet them, and bowed to the ground. "My lord," he said, "I beg you, if I find favour with you, kindly do not pass your servant by."* (18:2-3)

Abraham's hospitality to these three strangers by the Oak of Mamre is, in fact, an encounter with the living God, and brings with it future blessings for him and his wife. His openness to others is richly rewarded.

❖ Father, let me not turn in on myself out of grumpiness or fear. Help me to be open to people even if I find them hard to understand, or if they seem to think me stupid. Help me not to set limits on the people and places through which I am able to see your presence and action. I pray especially for (name your intention)

Our Father - Hail Mary - Glory Be

Fifth Day: *God said to Abraham, "As for Sarah your wife...I will bless her and moreover give you a son by her...kings of peoples shall descend from her." Abraham bowed to the ground, and he laughed, thinking to himself, "Is a child to be born to a man one hundred years old, and will Sarah have a child at the age of ninety?"* (17:15-17)

Abraham was called to persevere in trusting God - to faith. He thought it was too late for him to start a new life. But it is never too late to convert.

❖ Father, you know me. I have my sins and some of them are very ingrained. Help me not to despair of ever conquering them, but also not to become so used to them that I see them as part of me. Don't let me guard them jealously. It is never too late to convert. I pray especially for (name your intention)

Our Father - Hail Mary - Glory Be

Sixth Day: *Abraham remained standing before the Lord... he said "Are you really going to destroy the just man with the sinner? Perhaps there are fifty just men in the town. Will you really overwhelm them? ...Do not think of doing such a thing...will the judge of the whole earth not administer justice?"* (18:22-25)

When God tells Abraham he plans to destroy Sodom, a city notorious for wickedness and sexual violence, Abraham intercedes for the Sodomites. Perhaps they are not all bad; will not God spare them, rather than blot out the righteous?

❖ In my old age I am not useless to you. I can pray and offer my sufferings and frustrations. Abraham, like Christ, did not stand in judgement on the people of Sodom but prayed and interceded for them. Help me too to be someone who can talk with you and earnestly pray for the ills of the world. I pray especially for (name your intention)

Our Father - Hail Mary - Glory Be

Seventh Day: *The Lord dealt kindly with Sarah as he had said, and did what he had promised her. So Sarah conceived and bore a son to Abraham in his old age, at the time God had promised. Abraham named the son born to him Isaac, the son to whom Sarah had given birth...Abraham was a hundred years old when his son Isaac was born to him.* (21:1-3, 5)

Although Abraham's wife Sarah was understandably sceptical, God gave them a child in their old age. This event shows how God is generous and does what we cannot imagine possible; we need not think this should be understood only in terms of children in old age.

❖ Father, help me not to think that nothing new can happen to me in my old age; you can bring new life out of me when I am old, in some way I do not expect. I pray especially for (name your intention)

Our Father - Hail Mary - Glory Be

Eighth Day: *Now Sarah watched the son that Hagar the Egyptian had borne to Abraham, playing with her son Isaac. "Drive away that slave-girl and her son," she said to Abraham…This greatly distressed Abraham…but God said to him, "Do not distress yourself…Grant Sarah all she asks of you, for it is through Isaac that your name will be carried on. But the slave-girl's son I will also make into a nation, for he is your child too." Rising early next morning Abraham took some bread and a skin of water, and giving them to Hagar, he put the child on her shoulder and sent her away.* (21:9-14)

Before Abraham could fulfil the plan God had for him, he had to leave behind those parts of his past life that could have no part in what was to come. He was very reluctant to do this; but God assured him he would care for Hagar and her son, and Abraham believed and trusted him.

❖ Teach me to know what things I have to let go of in order to move on, and to trust you to take care of the things I can't. Give me discernment to know what these things are. I pray especially for (name your intention)

Our Father - Hail Mary - Glory Be

Ninth Day: *Isaac spoke to his father Abraham, "Father" he said…"Look…here are the fire and the wood, but where is the lamb for the burnt offering?" Abraham answered, "My son, God himself will provide the lamb"…Then looking up, Abraham saw a ram caught by its horns in a bush. Abraham took the ram and offered it as a burnt offering in place of his son.* (22:7-8, 13)

The sacrifice of Isaac shows how we must hand over to God everything we love most, full of faith that God will restore to us all things.

❖ Father, give me a Christian death and welcome me into the land you have promised me, knowing that you have already provided the Lamb of God to take away my sins. I pray especially for (name your intention)

Our Father - Hail Mary - Glory Be

Endnotes

[1] The official Latin equivalent is *novendialis prex*, "nine days' prayer".

[2] *Acts* 1.14.

[3] In 1897 Pope Leo XIII asked that this practice, which was of long custom, should be celebrated by all Catholics worldwide. The official *Handbook of Indulgences* states that "a *partial indulgence* is granted the Christian faithful who devoutly take part in a publicly celebrated novena before the solemnity of Christmas, Pentecost, or the Immaculate Conception of the Blessed Virgin Mary" (3rd edition 1986, English edition 1991, par.33 (p.72 in the edition published by the Catholic Book Publishing Corporation of New York)).

[4] This is primarily true of Jesus Christ: "The forty days of Jesus represent the forty years of Israel's wandering in the desert; the whole of Israel's history is concentrated in him….the history of Israel, which corresponds to our life's history, finds its ultimate meaning in the Passion that Jesus undergoes." Congregation for Divine Worship and the Discipline of the Sacraments, *Homiletic Directory*, par.59 (CTS, 2015, p.40).

[5] *On the Threshold of Transformation* (Chicago, Loyola Press, 2010), p.242.

A world of Catholic reading at your fingertips...

Catholic Faith, Life & Truth for all

www.CTSbooks.org

twitter: @CTSpublishers

facebook.com/CTSpublishers

Catholic Truth Society, Publishers to the Holy See.